YOUR WWII &
BLITZ

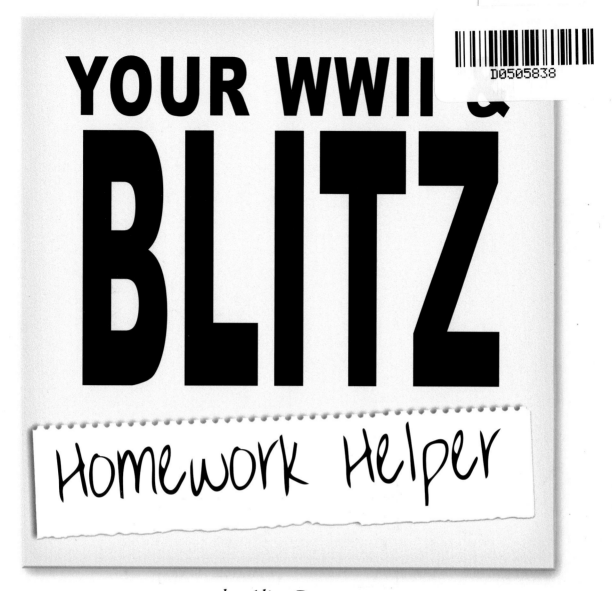

Homework Helper

by *Alice Proctor*
Consultant: *Alison Howard*

ticktock

501 310 219

How to use this book

Each topic in this book is clearly labelled and contains all these components:

Topic heading

Introduction to the topic

Sub-topic 1 offers complete information about one aspect of the topic

Choose a word from the Keyword Contents on page 3. Then, turn to the correct page and look for your word in BOLD CAPITALS. This will take you straight to the information you need

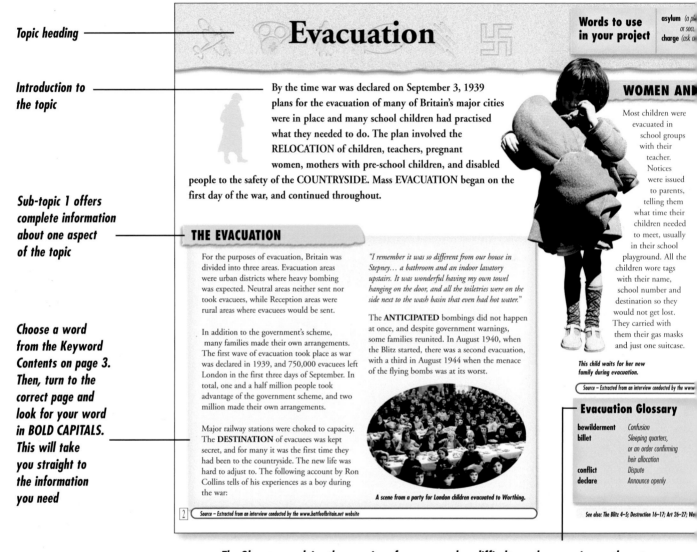

Words to use in your project

asylum *(a pl...*
or secu...
charge *(ask a...*

Evacuation

By the time war was declared on September 3, 1939 plans for the evacuation of many of Britain's major cities were in place and many school children had practised what they needed to do. The plan involved the RELOCATION of children, teachers, pregnant women, mothers with pre-school children, and disabled people to the safety of the COUNTRYSIDE. Mass EVACUATION began on the first day of the war, and continued throughout.

THE EVACUATION

For the purposes of evacuation, Britain was divided into three areas. Evacuation areas were urban districts where heavy bombing was expected. Neutral areas neither sent nor took evacuees, while Reception areas were rural areas where evacuees would be sent.

In addition to the government's scheme, many families made their own arrangements. The first wave of evacuation took place as war was declared in 1939, and 750,000 evacuees left London in the first three days of September. In total, one and a half million people took advantage of the government scheme, and two million made their own arrangements.

Major railway stations were choked to capacity. The **DESTINATION** of evacuees was kept secret, and for many it was the first time they had been to the countryside. The new life was hard to adjust to. The following account by Ron Collins tells of his experiences as a boy during the war:

"I remember it was so different from our house in Stepney... a bathroom and an indoor lavatory upstairs. It was wonderful having my own towel hanging on the door, and all the toiletries were on the side next to the wash basin that even had hot water."

The **ANTICIPATED** bombings did not happen at once, and despite government warnings, some families reunited. In August 1940, when the Blitz started, there was a second evacuation, with a third in August 1944 when the menace of the flying bombs was at its worst.

A scene from a party for London children evacuated to Worthing.

Source – Extracted from an interview conducted by the www.battleofbritain.net website

WOMEN AN...

Most children were evacuated in school groups with their teacher. Notices were issued to parents, telling them what time their children needed to meet, usually in their school playground. All the children wore tags with their name, school number and destination so they would not get lost. They carried with them their gas masks and just one suitcase.

This child waits for her new family during evacuation.

Source – Extracted from an interview conducted by the www

Evacuation Glossary

bewilderment	Confusion
billet	Sleeping quarters, or an order confirming heir allocation
conflict	Dispute
declare	Announce openly

See also: The Blitz 4–5; Destruction 16–17; Art 26–27; We...

The Glossary explains the meaning of any unusual or difficult words appearing on these two pages

Sub-topic 2 offers complete information about one aspect of the topic

Some suggested words to use in your project

The Case Study is a closer look at a famous person, artefact or building that relates to the topic

Captions clearly explain what is in the picture

Each photo or illustration is described and discussed in its accompanying text

Other pages in the book that relate to what you have read here are listed in this bar

At the bottom of some sections, a reference bar tells you where the quote has come from

(going out, especially in a large group) (suitcases, trunks)

refugee (a person who seeks shelter elsewhere, particularly in a time of war)

or hours omes.

d in the ge, they a hall d choose mes a host have been dren had ees, but ppy.
hard for others.
RP official reception

mothers was But the uite different.
tightly holding

a place

d in the

n of action for rticular object

CASE STUDY

Children having their feet inspected before evacuation.

Billets

As part of the preparation for evacuation, billeting officers found families in Reception areas who were willing to take in evacuees. Many people volunteered to take the city children. They received 10s 6d (10 shillings and sixpence, or about 52p) from the government for one child, and 8s 6d (about 42p) for each extra child. This was for accommodation and food, but the child's parents were responsible for clothing. High unemployment in the 1930s meant that many children from poor city areas had only the clothes they arrived in and had not been fed properly. As a result, the government issued free school milk, and cod liver oil for children under five.

Evelyn Rose was evacuated from her London home when war broke out:

"I was fourteen when war was declared. We were billeted with a family in a large house where there were servants. It was not something that we were used to."

Source – Voices from the Past: The Blitz (1987) 3

Keyword Contents

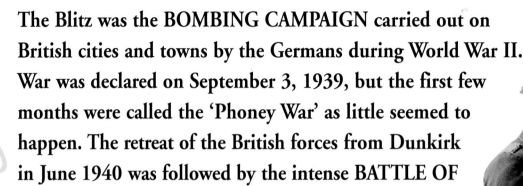

The Blitz

The Blitz was the BOMBING CAMPAIGN carried out on British cities and towns by the Germans during World War II. War was declared on September 3, 1939, but the first few months were called the 'Phoney War' as little seemed to happen. The retreat of the British forces from Dunkirk in June 1940 was followed by the intense BATTLE OF BRITAIN fought in the skies over southern Britain until September 1940. The Blitz then began, and lasted until May 1941.

THE BOMBINGS

The Blitz (a shortening of the German word *Blitzkrieg,* or 'lightning war') was a period of devastating bombing of London and other major British towns and cities, including Coventry and Southampton. After war was declared, British and French troops fought the Germans in mainland Europe, but were pushed back. Germany took over France and planned to invade Britain. The Battle of Britain stopped this plan, so the Germans changed tactic and started the Blitz campaign.

From 4pm on September 7, 1940, London was attacked for two hours by 348 German **BOMBERS** escorted by 617 fighters. There was a second attack two hours later, and this time the targets could be seen by the fires left blazing after the first assault. This went on throughout the night. Over the next 57 days, London was bombed every day or night. The resulting fires devastated huge areas of the city.

The Blitz ended on May 10, 1941 when Adolf Hitler ordered his bombers to prepare for Germany's invasion of Russia. Wartime correspondent Ernie Pyle describes a night raid on London in 1940:

"They came just after dark, and somehow you could sense from the quick, bitter firing of the guns that there was to be no monkey business this night. Shortly after the sirens wailed you could hear the Germans grinding overhead."

The first mass air raid on London, September 7, 1940.

Source – A Dreadful Masterpiece, Ernie's War: The Best of Ernie Pyle's World War II Dispatches (1986)

Words to use in your project

Axis powers *(alliance between Germany, Italy and Japan during World War II)*
casualty *(dead or injured person)*
command *(to order, demand, or exercise control over)*
infrastructure *(basic framework, system of communications)*
rationing *(limiting food supply)*

THE LUFTWAFFE

The Luftwaffe (pronounced 'looft-vaaf-feh') was the German air force. The name means 'air weapon'. At the start of the war in 1939 the Luftwaffe was the world's most powerful air force. From the start of the war until June 1940, the German forces invaded Belgium, Denmark, France, Luxembourg, the Netherlands, Norway, Poland and Sweden. Much of the success was attributed to the Luftwaffe.

Luftwaffe Commander Hermann Goring (left) with Ernst Udet, who chose the force's planes.

When attention turned to Britain, Hermann Göring, head of the Luftwaffe, thought it would take only a month to subdue the RAF. But the Luftwaffe met fierce resistance, so its planes were sent to **DESTROY** major British cities and towns from Aberdeen to Plymouth, and particularly London. Adolf Hitler's Directive No. 16 from July 16, 1940 states:

'Since Britain still shows no sign of willingness to come to an agreement in spite of her hopeless military situation, I have decided to prepare and if necessary carry out an amphibious operation against England… to eliminate the English mother country as a base for continuation of the war against Germany and, if it should become necessary, to occupy the entire island.'

Sources – Operation Seelöwe (Sea Lion), Directive No. 16, July 16, 1940

The Blitz Glossary

amphibious	On water	**invade**	Enter and take over a country with an armed force
assault	Attack		
bombard	In warfare, a relentless onslaught	**subdue**	Overcome or bring under control
correspondent	Reporter	**tactic**	A system or element of skilled or calculated operations
directive	An official or authorative instruction	**warfare**	Military operations

See also: The Raids 6–7; Evacuation 8–9; Shelters 12–13; Significant People 24–25

CASE STUDY

RAF Spitfires (above) and Hurricanes proved superior aircraft to the German fighters in the Battle of Britain.

Battle of Britain

Britain had developed radar to detect approaching enemy planes, and had built more than 50 radar bases. The Germans **TARGETED** these key points, along with airfields and plane factories, in their bid to destroy Britain's Royal Air Force (RAF) in preparation for an **INVASION** they planned called Operation Sea Lion.

In July 1940, Germany's air force, the Luftwaffe, began its attack. It had more aircraft and trained pilots, but radar, as well as more than 1,000 observation posts, provided the RAF with vital information about what the Germans were doing. The RAF also had better planes than the Luftwaffe. Pilots from Poland, France and other countries flew with the RAF, which lost 792 planes in the next three months. The Luftwaffe lost nearly twice as many. In September 1940, Winston Churchill praised the 3,080 pilots who had defended Britain:

"Never, in the field of human conflict, has so much, been owed by so many, to so few!"

Source – Speech by Churchill, August 20, 1940

5

The Raids

Luftwaffe attacks during the Battle of Britain left the RAF on the point of collapse. In just another 24 hours it would probably have been defeated. Then Göring made a mistake: he ordered the Luftwaffe to target other towns and cities, which gave the RAF time to repair its planes and regroup. The Blitz had started.

The Luftwaffe made 127 large-scale NIGHT RAIDS on Britain's towns and cities between September 1940 and May 1941, 71 of them on London. The attacks were designed to destroy important buildings, and to demoralise people.

LONDON

London was the most heavily **BOMBED** British city during the Blitz. The Luftwaffe targeted industrial areas, major ports, factories and transport links. When the Luftwaffe targeted the docks it put people living in east London and near the River Thames in the firing line. The raids began on September 7, 1940 with a daylight raid on London's East End, dropping incendiary bombs that started more than 1,000 fires. The fires were still burning that night, which allowed the German bombers to see their **TARGETS**. The bombings continued every night for a further 75 nights, and the raids broadened to cover central London and the suburbs. More than 18,000 tons of bombs were dropped on London – more than were dropped on the whole of the rest of Britain. The raids began again, and continued until May. More than 20,000 Londoners died and 1.4 million were made homeless. In his autobiography, Kingsley Martin, wrote:

"In the West End, we could 'take' the raids we got; whether we could have survived many more like the last two raids in the spring of 1941....I don't know... but... bombs do not induce surrender."

A typical scene of East End life in London, 1940. Life continued despite the raids.

Sources – Kingsley Martin, Father Figures (1966)

Words to use in your project

Barbarossa *(code name for the German invasion of the Soviet Union in June 1941)*

fighter-bomber *(a fighter and a bomber aircraft, used in tactical and defensive operations)*

reconnaissance *(survey to seek out information about enemy position or installations)*

OTHER TARGETS

The main targets outside London were Belfast, Birmingham, Bristol, Cardiff, Coventry, Glasgow, Hull, Liverpool, Manchester, Newcastle, Nottingham, Portsmouth, Plymouth, Sheffield and Southampton. All had some significant industrial or wartime purpose that the Germans wanted to disable.

The Blitz Memorial in Liverpool. It reads: "In loving memory of the Citizens of Liverpool and Bootle who lost their lives in the Blitz of 1940-42."

But sometimes a bomber that had missed its target drop zone or had met some other problem would simply drop bombs at random, so innocent civilians were often **CASUALTIES**. The Baedeker Raids on historic cities such as Bath and York in 1942, and the V1 and V2 (flying bomb) **ROCKET CAMPAIGNS** later in the war meant that Britain's population was always on the alert and unsure when they could be bombed. Publisher Leonard Woolf, the husband of the famous novelist Virginia, lived in Rodmell, Sussex at the start of the war, and wrote:

'The strange first air raid of the war... It came, I think, just after or before breakfast and I walked out onto the lawn which looks over the water-meadows to Lewes and the Downs.'

Sources – Leonard Woolf, The Journey Not the Arrival Matters (1969)

The Raids Glossary

autobiography	Account of a person's life written by the subject	**explosive**	Likely to shatter violently or burst apart
casualty	Dead or injured person	**incendiary**	Designed to cause fires
consecutive	One after the other	**morale**	Confidence or optimism in a person or a group
devastate	Lay waste, demolish		
disable	Render inactive	**target**	An object to be attacked

CASE STUDY

Coventry Cathedral – only the tower and outer walls remain intact today.

Blitz on Coventry

The worst devastation outside London was in Coventry, home of some large manufacturing companies that made planes and other essential war items. The factories had been relocated to the edge of Coventry to reduce the risk to residential areas. The city had already been bombed during the summer and autumn of 1940. At 7.20pm on November 14, the first of 500 German bombers dropped parachute flares followed by **INCENDIARIES** to mark the way for the main force of bombers. Within 10 minutes, the second wave of bombers arrived and dropped high explosive bombs. A newspaper reported:

"The spire of Coventry Cathedral to-day stood as a sentinel over the grim scene of destruction following a dusk-to-dawn raid on the town which the Nazis claimed was the biggest attack in the history of air war."

Source – The Guardian, November 16, 1940

See also: The Blitz 4–5; Defence 10–11; After the Raids 14–15; Women and Children 22–23

Evacuation

By the time war was declared on September 3, 1939 plans for the evacuation of many of Britain's major cities were in place and many school children had practised what they needed to do. The plan involved the **RELOCATION** of children, teachers, pregnant women, mothers with pre-school children, and disabled people to the safety of the **COUNTRYSIDE**. Mass **EVACUATION** began on the first day of the war, and continued throughout.

THE EVACUATION

For the purposes of evacuation, Britain was divided into three areas. Evacuation areas were urban districts where heavy bombing was expected. Neutral areas neither sent nor took evacuees, while Reception areas were rural areas where evacuees would be sent.

In addition to the government's scheme, many families made their own arrangements. The first wave of evacuation took place as war was declared in 1939, and 750,000 evacuees left London in the first three days of September. In total, one and a half million people took advantage of the government scheme, and two million made their own arrangements.

Major railway stations were choked to capacity. The **DESTINATION** of evacuees was kept secret, and for many it was the first time they had been to the countryside. The new life was hard to adjust to. The following account by Ron Collins tells of his experiences as a boy during the war:

"I remember it was so different from our house in Stepney… a bathroom and an indoor lavatory upstairs. It was wonderful having my own towel hanging on the door, and all the toiletries were on the side next to the wash basin that even had hot water."

The **ANTICIPATED** bombings did not happen at once, and despite government warnings, some families reunited. In August 1940, when the Blitz started, there was a second evacuation, with a third in August 1944 when the menace of the flying bombs was at its worst.

A scene from a party for London children evacuated to Worthing.

Source – Extracted from an interview conducted by the www.battleofbritain.net website

Words to use in your project

asylum *(a place of safety or security)*
charge *(ask as a price or fee)*
exodus *(going out, especially in a large group)*
luggage *(suitcases, trunks)*
refugee *(a person who seeks shelter elsewhere, particularly in a time of war)*

WOMEN AND CHILDREN

Most children were evacuated in school groups with their teacher. Notices were issued to parents, telling them what time their children needed to meet, usually in their school playground. All the children wore tags with their name, school number and destination so they would not get lost. They carried with them their gas masks and just one suitcase.

This child waits for her new family during evacuation.

Many had to travel for hours to get to their new homes.

When children arrived in the **HOST** town or village, they might be lined up in a hall so host families could choose one of them. Sometimes a host family would already have been arranged. Many children had happy times as evacuees, but some were very unhappy. Evacuation was very hard for both children and mothers. George Clarke, an ARP official at the Bethnal Green reception point, wrote:

'The feelings amongst the mothers was generally quite orderly, ... But the children's behaviour was quite different. Some remained very quiet tightly holding onto mum's hand ...'

Source – Extracted from an interview conducted by the www.battleofbritain.net website

Evacuation Glossary

bewilderment	Confusion	**evacuate**	Remove from a place
billet	Sleeping quarters, or an order confirming their allocation	**lavatory**	Toilet
		pregnant	Carrying a child in the womb
conflict	Dispute	**scheme**	Systematic plan of action for attaining a particular object
declare	Announce openly		

See also: The Blitz 4–5; Destruction 16–17; Art 26–27; Weapons 28–29; Crime 30–31

CASE STUDY

Children having their feet inspected before evacuation.

Billets

As part of the preparation for evacuation, billeting officers found families in Reception areas who were willing to take in evacuees. Many people volunteered to take the city children. They received 10s 6d (10 shillings and sixpence, or about 52p) from the government for one child, and 8s 6d (about 42p) for each extra child. This was for accommodation and food, but the child's parents were responsible for clothing. High unemployment in the 1930s meant that many children from poor city areas had only the clothes they arrived in and had not been fed properly. As a result, the government issued free school milk, and cod liver oil for children under five.

Evelyn Rose was evacuated from her London home when war broke out:

"I was fourteen when war was declared. We were billeted with a family in a large house where there were servants. It was not something that we were used to."

Source – Voices from the Past: The Blitz (1987)

9

Defence

Britain's defence was the responsibility of the armed services working with the emergency services and various volunteer organisations. The early WARNING RADAR system, anti-aircraft guns, searchlights and barrage balloons were used to combat bombing raids. A vital role was played by the Observer Corps (later The Royal Observer Corps), and more than 1,000 units in coastal areas provided information on impending attacks. Air raid sirens could then be sounded, and ground and air defences notified.

MILITARY DEFENCE

Anti-aircraft guns were set up all over London and in other strategic locations. They were manned by specially trained crews whose job was to **SHOOT** down **ENEMY** planes, or to try to prevent the planes attacking. Searchlights were used to scan the night sky to help the gunners spot enemy planes and keep them in their sights.

Barrage balloons were enormous silvery balloons. They were flown over the countryside to **PREVENT** planes from flying low or dive-bombing. A plane that hit the balloon or its supporting cable would crash. It took about 16 people to launch or bring down a balloon, which was wound into position on a winch. The winch could be raised or lowered as needed. Balloons could be anchored to the ground or to the back of a large lorry, so they were easy to move around.

Harold Nicolson, who was National Liberal MP for West Leicester from 1935 to 1945, wrote in his diary on September 1, 1939:

"Motor up... to London. When we get near London we see a row of balloons hanging like black spots in the air. Go down to the House of Commons at 5.30. They have already darkened the building and lowered the lights... I am startled to find a perfectly black city."

A cluster of Royal Air Force barrage balloons at Cardington.

Source – Harold Nicolson, diary entry, 1st September, 1939

CIVIL DEFENCE

A WWII air raid siren.

Arrangements to protect civilians in war are known as civil defence. The war on the Home Front, as

Cadet Corps. First aid teams, fire-watchers, firefighters and rescue parties were trained in conjunction with the emergency services (fire, police and ambulance). During London's Blitz, they fought fires caused by bombing and rescued people from bombed buildings.

Air Raid Wardens worked in teams of about six. Each warden took care of several streets and dealt with the **CONSEQUENCES** of bombs dropped in that area. This excerpt is from *Air Raid Warnings*, a 1939 British government circular:

Britain was known, involved air-raid **PRECAUTIONS** (ARP) the Royal Observer Corps which carried out duties including plane-spotting, and the Civil Defence

'When air raids are threatened, warning will be given in towns by sirens and hooters... When you hear the warning, take cover at once... Stay under cover until you hear the sirens sounding continuously for two minutes on the same note...'

Source – Extract from a British government circular Air Raid Warnings (1939)

Defence Glossary

barrage	A barrier	**rescue**	Save from a dangerous or distressing situation
hood	A covering		
impending	About to happen	**restriction**	Limitation
patrol	A person or group sent to keep watch over an area	**siren**	A device that produces a loud sound, used as a warning
reinforce	Strengthen (in wartime, with additional troops)	**strategic**	Relating to military tactics

CASE STUDY

Government advertising posters told people what to do during the blackout.

The Blackout

Even before war was declared it was realised that lights in towns, cities and other strategic locations should be hidden or put out to stop the Luftwaffe using them to guide them to their targets.

The BLACKOUT came into force half an hour after sunset until half an hour before sunrise. All outside lights, including street lamps, had to be switched off, and all windows and doors had to be covered so that no light at all could be seen. Car headlights had only a tiny slit that pointed downwards, and even torches and bicycle lamps had special hoods. A British government circular from July 1939 described the blackout law:

"All windows, skylights, glazed doors, or other openings which would show a light, will have to be screened... with dark blinds... or brown paper pasted on the glass, so that no light is visible from outside."

Source – Extract from government circular, 1939

See also: The Raids 6–7; Food and Farming 18–19; Work and Play 20–21; Weapons 28–29

Shelters

There were two kinds of shelters for home use: the Anderson shelter and the Morrison shelter. In public areas, shelters were often below the ground, and in London the UNDERGROUND railway or Tube was used. When night bombing raids were at their height late in 1940, many people slept in shelters every night, and underground stations were kitted out with beds, toilets, first aid facilities and even CANTEENS. Public shelters were policed by Shelter Marshals.

HOME SHELTERS

The government was worried that when the bombing started people would go into public shelters and be too scared to come out. It was also aware that a bomb hitting a large public shelter could result in more deaths, so it encouraged people to live their lives as normally as possible and issued families with free shelters.

Anderson shelters, probably named after Home Secretary John Anderson, came first. They were constructed from **CORRUGATED** metal and had to be dug 1.2 metres into the ground and covered with soil. They were put up in gardens and people often grew vegetables on top of them. They were effective, but when it rained they were very damp and could flood. Around 2,250,000 Anderson shelters were given out. An alternative, introduced late in 1940, was the Morrison indoor shelter. This was a large metal frame about 2 metres long and 1.2 metres wide, with wire walls. It took up a lot

of room but could also be used as a dining table. It was very effective, and saved many lives.

Muriel Sybil Ward lived in East London for more than thirty years until 1948:

"…although I left home during the winter in the dark, at least I was able to get back in the daylight and eat before the air raid warning sounded. My mother and I slept in an Anderson air raid shelter in the garden most nights… My father only joined us if things 'got bad'!"

An Anderson Shelter erected in January 1940.

Sources – Extract from the memoirs of Muriel Sybil Ward, born in 1916

Words to use in your project

alarm (*a signal, sound, cry, etc. that is a warning of danger*)

council (*a group of people called together for consultation*)

disorder (*an upset of normal function*)

household (*the home and its affairs*)

sanctuary (*a place of refuge*)

GOING UNDERGROUND

At the peak of the Blitz, 79 underground stations became shelters, and up to 177,000 Londoners slept in them each night. Though they were considered safe, there were many deaths when stations including Bank and Balham took direct hits. Bombs could cause damage up to 15 metres underground, and not all stations were that deep. Flooding was a risk if a water main above was hit.

The London Underground was also used by the government and the armed services. Special offices were built in disused **PASSAGES** and at some stations. The War Cabinet met in a secret Tube shelter to escape the bombing, and Anti-Aircraft Control used a disused station as its **HEADQUARTERS**.

Evelyn Rose describes the underground shelters:

'I did not like using them myself. The stench was unbearable. The smell was so bad I don't know how people did not die from suffocation. So many bodies and no fresh air coming in.'

A reconstruction of a wartime London underground shelter.

Sources – Extracted from an interview conducted by the www.battleofbritain.net website

Shelters Glossary

armband	Cloth band worn round the upper arm	**shelter**	Something that protects
construct	Build	**singsong**	A monotonous type of singing
corrugate	Ridged and grooved	**suffocation**	Death through lack of air
encourage	promote	**underground**	Beneath the surface
regulations	Sets of rules	**unhygenic**	Not clean

CASE STUDY

A crowded scene in a air raid shelter. A Shelter Marshal and two young men are playing the harmonica.

Shelter Marshals

Shelter Marshals kept order in public **AIR-RAID** shelters. With so many anxious people together in cramped and unhygienic conditions arguments could soon break out. They were also there to give first aid, and to deal with problems like flooding in the deep level shelters. Londoners using Tube stations for overnight shelter often turned up well before the sirens went off to secure a good spot, and this could cause disagreements.

Marshals wore the initials SM on a white armband and on their tin helmet. Dolly Rolph, a deputy warden in shelters in Bethnal Green, saw some DISCIPLINE problems. Some of those taking shelter brought in a piano and began to have noisy singsongs that kept other people awake. She had to ask the local council to bring in regulations to restrict noise. She said: 'They were 'lively times.'

Source – Interview conducted by the www.battleofbritain.net

Sirens sounded the 'all clear' to tell people it was safe to leave their shelters. For many it was a time to survey the DAMAGE as they found their homes and businesses flattened, or worse – dead or injured relatives and friends. The Luftwaffe dropped bombs that exploded on impact, and also used incendiary and delayed-action bombs that could kill or injure after the raid was over. Fighting fires, RESCUING people and making buildings safe kept the police, firefighters, ambulance drivers and ARP wardens busy.

FIRE FIGHTING

The Civil Defence Act of 1937 made it possible for local authorities to recruit an Auxiliary Fire Service (AFS) to support the main Fire Brigade. By the start of the war in September 1939, 23,000 members had trained, mobilised and equipped in London alone, and more than 300 Auxiliary Fire Service stations established.

Winston Churchill referred to the brave firefighters who took such risks during the Blitz as '**HEROES** with grimy faces'. In London, more than 800 firefighters lost their lives.

Large engines manned by teams of firefighters were dispatched to big fires, but it was soon realised that smaller **EQUIPMENT** was needed. This would be easier to transport quickly to where it was needed before the fire could spread. Many London taxis were converted to pull a small **TENDER**. The Soap Box Fire Engine was made from cardboard boxes mounted on pram wheels and equipped with hand pumps, sandbags and water buckets.

ARP posts had basic but effective apparatus, to combat fires caused by incendiary bombs. It was usually a bucket for water and a stirrup pump, as well as sand to throw over the fire.

This extract is from the memoirs of a London firefighter in the Docklands during Blitz:

"There were pepper fires ... There were rum fires ... There was a paint fire ... A rubber fire gave forth black clouds of smoke that could only be fought from a distance, always threatening to choke the attackers."

Firefighters at work in a bomb-damaged street after a Saturday night raid in 1941.

Source – Alan P. Herbert, Memories of the Forties (1965)

EMERGENCY SERVICES

It was the job of Civil Defence workers to clear up the carnage after air raids. Teams including firemen, ambulance crew and stretcher-bearers went to the aid of those trapped or wounded by bombs. It could be difficult to find survivors trapped under rubble, and complete silence was needed to hear any cries for help. Buildings could collapse at any time. There was also a risk from burst water or gas mains and unexploded bombs.

If an unexploded bomb was found, the army's **BOMB DISPOSAL UNIT** would undertake the risky job of removing its fuse.

In 1945, TP Peters, an Air Raid Warden in East Grinstead, wrote about his experiences:

'Unexploded German bombs were very dangerous. The Chief Warden and I would go and inspect the holes armed with rods, to enable him to fill up the necessary forms, etc, for the Bomb Disposal Unit.'

Respirators were handed during raids by Civil Defence workers.

Source – Reminiscences, TP Peters, (1945)

After the Raids Glossary

ambulance	Vehicle for carrying the sick	**mobilise**	Prepare and organise for active service
borough	A term for a town, and also a district of London	**mount**	Place on top of
apparatus	Equipment needed for a particular activity or purpose	**recruit**	Enlist
		survey	Examine carefully and thoroughly
carnage	The killing of many people	**tender**	Wheeled trailer
dispose	To get rid of		

See also: The Shelters 12–13; The Destruction 16–17; Work and Play 20–21; Significant People 24–25

A young air-raid warden in uniform.

Air-Raid Warden

Each borough in London had teams of ARP wardens working together to make sure that every street was covered. One in six ARP wardens was a woman. Wardens worked at least 72 hours a week, maintaining the blackout and checking that people were carrying their gas masks. Other duties included sounding sirens for air-raids and the 'all clear', fighting fires, giving first aid and dealing with unexploded bombs after a raid. The pay was £3 5s (£3.25) a week for men and £2 3s 6d (£2. 32) for women. At the height of the Blitz, many worked longer hours even though there was no overtime pay.

Air Raid Warden TP Peters wrote:

"When the Prime Minister announced the Declaration of War ... the country was well prepared with its ARP Organisation. We had received a good training from Colonel Eaton, the Chief Warden."

Source – TP Peters, Reminiscences (1945)

Destruction

During the Blitz, the loss of life and destruction to buildings was IMMENSE. In the first two months it is thought that more than a million bombs were dropped over Britain's skies. On the first night of the London Blitz more than 400 civilians were killed and 16,000 injured. About two million houses (more than a million of these in London) were DESTROYED, 60,000 CIVILIANS killed and 87,000 more seriously INJURED. Until half-way through World War II, more women and children in Britain had been killed than soldiers.

CASUALTIES

Although the Luftwaffe targeted military and industrial sites **ESSENTIAL** to Britain's war effort, civilian targets were also struck. This was partly an attempt to demoralise the British people, but it failed.

Many civilians were killed when bombs hit public shelters, especially in the early days of the Blitz when some shelters were not well built. On September 9, 1940, the *Manchester Guardian* reported what happened when a bomb fell inside an underground shelter:

"Children sleeping in perambulators and mothers with babies in their arms were killed when a bomb exploded on a crowded shelter in an East London district during Saturday night's raids. By what is described as "a million-to-one chance" the bomb fell directly on to a ventilator shaft measuring only about three feet by one foot."

All kinds of buildings were damaged or destroyed, including shops, businesses, schools, churches, cinemas and hospitals. The centre of

Coventry was completely flattened after a raid on November 14, 1940. The docks in London, Southampton, Portsmouth and Liverpool were also targets. Southampton had 2,300 bombs and more than 30,000 incendiary devices dropped on it, damaging and destroying 45,000 buildings, and it was reported that the glow from the fires could be seen in Cherbourg in northern France.

Plaque at Bethnal Green Tube Station. On March 3, 1943, 173 people lost their lives in the worst civilian tragedy of the war at Bethnal Green Tube station.

Sources – Manchester Guardian, September 9, 1940

SITES AND STRUCTURES

To **PROTECT** buildings, and those living and working in them, many were piled high on the outside with sandbags. Windows were covered

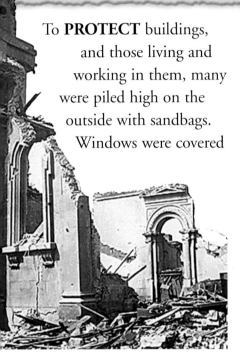

An old building wrecked after fire bombs and high explosives rained on the capital for many hours in April, 1941.

in tape to stop shattered glass forming **LETHAL** flying splinters. Buildings such as large factories or churches that could be reference points for Luftwaffe **NAVIGATORS** were covered in

CAMOUFLAGE netting or even painted.

The final big bombing raid of the Blitz, and one of the worst, took place on London on May 10, 1941. The Chamber of the House of Commons was destroyed and the House of Lords damaged when the Houses of Parliament were hit. All the **MAJOR** railway stations were damaged, as well as Westminster Abbey, St James's Palace, Lambeth Palace, the British Museum and the Central Criminal Court (Old Bailey). Tom Hopkinson wrote:

'Bombing for that year ended with the extremely heavy raid of May 10-11 in which it seemed the Germans were trying to burn down the whole of London at the same time.'

Source – Tom Hopkinson, Of This Our Time (1982)

The Destruction Glossary

commercial	Connected with trade	**spectacle**	A visually striking performance or display
demoralise	Destroy morale		
extinguish	Put out	**stupendous**	Extremely impressive
horrific	Filled with or causing horror	**uncontrollable**	Not under command
perambulator	A baby carriage with four wheels	**ventilator**	A device or appliance for ventilating a room or other space

See also: The Raids 6–7; After the Raids 14–15; Food and Farming 18–19; Art 26–27; Crime 30–31

CASE STUDY

London burns during the Blitz.

London ablaze

On December 29, 1940, the Luftwaffe attacked London. In two hours, it dropped about 100,000 incendiary bombs that started 1,500 fires. Almost all the fires were in central London so damage to shops and businesses was extremely high and 163 people were killed. Firefighters worked round the clock, and used an estimated 100 million gallons of water to put out the blazes. St Paul's Cathedral was struck by a bomb that destroyed its altar and damaged the crypt.

In his book *Memories of the Forties*, Alan P Herbert wrote:

"The Pool, below London Bridge, was a lake of light. I saw a stupendous spectacle. Half a mile or more of the Surrey shore was burning ... The scene was like a lake in Hell. Burning barges were drifting everywhere ... so dense was the smoke."

Source – Memories of the Forties, Alan P Herbert (1965)

Food and Farming

Before the war, Britain imported about 55 million tons of food plus other SUPPLIES every year. One of Germany's TACTICS was to cut off these much-needed supplies by destroying Britain's merchant navy which carried the provisions, usually across the Atlantic Ocean. As food IMPORTS declined because of the attacks, the British government developed two strategies. One was rationing, so that everyone received the same amount of food. The other was to encourage everyone to produce food and to support farming.

RATIONING AND SHORTAGES

Food rationing was introduced so that everyone received a fair share of food. **PRICES** were fixed at a standard rate so there was no over-charging. In January 1940, **RATIONING** was introduced. Even the Royal family had to adhere to it, though people who grew or raised things to eat had more food. Others made money on what is called the black market by selling goods **ILLEGALLY**.

Every family had to register with local shops to buy food. Sugar and bacon were rationed first, and each person's ration was only four ounces of each per week. As the war went on the list of rationed food became longer. Some things, including oranges and bananas, were not available at all. Eggs were usually sold in powdered form. Soon, more things were rationed, including petrol, coal and other materials needed for the war. People were encouraged to 'make do and mend' clothes and other items, but in June 1941 clothes rationing began. Utility furniture, which was basic but well-made, was introduced in 1943.

1940	Jan	Bacon
	Jan	Sugar
	March	Meat
	July	Tea
	July	Butter and margarine
1941	March	Jam
	May	Cheese
	June	Eggs
1942	January	Rice and dried fruit
	February	Canned tomatoes and peas
	April	Breakfast cereals and condensed milk
	July	Chocolate and sweets
	August	Biscuits
	December	Oat flakes

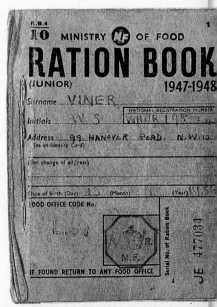

Rationing lasted from 1940-1954.

Words to use in your project

allocate *(to distribute in shares or according to a plan)*
cargo *(the load of commodities*

carried by a ship or airplane)
cultivate *(use soil or land for growing crops)*

decadent *(in a state of decline)*
emaciated *(to become abnormally lean by starvation)*

PRODUCING FOOD

In 1939 farming joined the war effort. The 'Dig for Victory' campaign encouraged people with gardens to produce as much food as possible. Those without a garden could have an **ALLOTMENT**, and in time more than 1,400,000 people had one. Food was grown everywhere, including parks, school playing fields, railway embankments, cricket pitches and even Buckingham Palace's flower beds. The campaign even had its own song:

Allotments in Greenwich Park during the war.

'Dig! Dig! Dig! And your muscles will grow big Keep on pushing the spade
Don't mind the worms
Just ignore their squirms
And when your back aches laugh with glee
And keep on diggin'
'Til we give our foes a wiggin'
Dig! Dig! Dig! to Victory'

| Sources – Ministry of Agriculture campaign, 1940 |

Food and Farming Glossary

adhere	*Stick fast*	**modernised**	*Brought up to date*
allotment	*A small patch of ground used for growing food*	**propaganda**	*Promotion of particular ideas*
campaign	*A series of organised, planned actions*	**ration**	*Allocate a fixed amount of a commodity that is in short supply*
coupon	*Detachable ticket, entitling bearer to set amount of food*	**relevant**	*Suitable*
		restricted	*Confined*

See also: Evacuation 8–9; Work and Play 20–21; Significant People 24–25; Art 26–27

CASE STUDY

A woman uses her ration book during the war.

Food Inspectors

During rationing work people were given books of COUPONS to hand over when they went to buy food. Food Inspectors checked that shopkeepers did not sell goods without taking the right coupons. Sometimes they worked undercover, and one way they did this was to pretend to be a customer. She would hand over her ration book and ask for one ration of meat. When the shopkeeper had almost finished serving, the Inspector would change her mind and ask for more meat. If the shopkeeper forgot to remove another coupon, he would be charged with breaking rationing restrictions. According to the *East Grinstead Observer* (September 16, 1944):

"Dr Frederick Ridley of Mudbrooks Farm, Forest Row, was found guilty of adding water to milk for sale. Dr Ridley was fined £15 and £3 3s costs."

| Source – East Grinstead Observer Sept 16, 1944 |

Work and Play

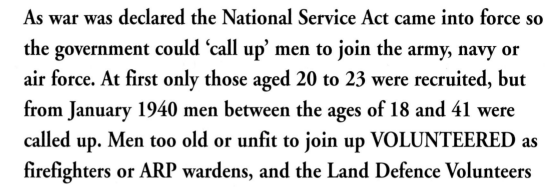

As war was declared the National Service Act came into force so the government could 'call up' men to join the army, navy or air force. At first only those aged 20 to 23 were recruited, but from January 1940 men between the ages of 18 and 41 were called up. Men too old or unfit to join up VOLUNTEERED as firefighters or ARP wardens, and the Land Defence Volunteers or Home Guard ('Dad's Army') was ESTABLISHED. Some important jobs were 'reserved occupations' so the men who did them were not called up.

THE BLITZ SPIRIT

It was feared that people would stay at home during the war and cause problems for employers. Quite the opposite happened, however, as many Londoners were determined to maintain "business as usual". As well as serving in the armed forces, many other important roles emerged. Traditionally men had worked in factories, driven lorries and farmed land, but now they were fighting, women took on these roles. Boys and girls in the Scouts and Guides did a range of important jobs from delivering urgent messages to making clothes for the soldiers. Princess Elizabeth (now Queen Elizabeth II) registered for war work three days after her 16th birthday in 1942 as was required by the government, and in 1945 she joined the ATS (Auxiliary Transport Service) and qualified as a driver and mechanic.

London's Bishopsgate Institute's librarian reported to his committee in October 1940 that:

"'Two members of staff – Miss Reid and Miss Daniels – have had to evacuate their homes in Stepney owing to the serous damage caused by bombs; but I am happy to state that beyond shock they are well and have loyally attended to their duties here'."

Daily life in a damaged residential neighbourhood.

Source – Bishopsgate Institue Committee Report, October 1940

Words to use in your project

attire *(to dress in fine garments)*
customary *(in keeping with custom)*

enlist *(to enroll for service in armed forces)*

entertainment *(something that gives pleasure)*
explanation *(making things clear)*

PASTIMES

Despite the difficulties, reading, listening to music, the cinema, the arts and going to see plays or a concert remained hugely **POPULAR**. The BBC had stopped broadcasting television when war broke out, so most people either read a newspaper or listened to the radio to find out the news. Cinemas showed newsreels as well as films. Disney was becoming popular and Snow White being released just before the war. CEMA was the Council for the Encouragement of Music and the Arts, and it organised all sort of cultural events and concerts, including special **ENTERTAINMENTS** for factory workers. Cheap paperbacks, introduced first by Penguin Books, meant that there was something to do and a way to escape the boredom and discomfort of long train journeys or sheltering during air raids.

Dances, singing and sports competitions were popular, not least because they helped the **COMMUNITY SPIRIT**.

Paperback books became a popular diversion from the hardships of the war in Britain.

CASE STUDY

The Windmill was the only London theatre that remained open throughout the Blitz.

Theatre

People used the theatre as a way of forgetting their problems. Many actors and backstage workers had been called up. The blackout meant that performances were held in late afternoon or early evening and rationing affected the availability of costumes and make-up. Signs were used during a performance to warn of an air raid. **AUDIENCE** members could leave if they wanted, but most people chose to stay watching the play. In London's famous West End, troops made up a large part of the audience until the early summer of 1941 when they were banned from taking their leave in London.

Theatre World wrote about these problems in its October 1940 issue:

"The choice of the Londoner is now restricted to the delights of the Revudeville at the Windmill and the lunch-time ballet hour at the Arts Theatre Club, to which must be added the brave venture of Shakespeare at the Vaudeville, matinees only."

Work and Play Glossary

competitions	Striving to gain or win something by defeating others	**morale**	Mental condition with respect to courage
decorating	To add something to so as to make more attractive	**newsreel**	Short film of recent events
entertainment	Recreation	**vaudeville**	Form of variety entertainment
matinee	Afternoon cinema show	**volunteer**	A person who chooses freely to do a given task

See also: The Blitz 4–5; Shelters 12–13; Food and Farming 18–19; Women and Children 22–23

Source – Theatre World, October 1940

Women and Children

When men were called up to fight, it left a shortage of workers in traditionally male occupations, such as farming and factory work. In 1939 the Women's Land Army began to ask for volunteers and by 1944 about 80,000 women were working on farms. In 1941, women aged between 19 and 30 had to register for war work and many became drivers, mechanics or worked in MUNITIONS factories. The Women's Voluntary Service (WVS) provided meals and CLOTHING for rescue workers and those who survived air raids.

WORKING WOMEN

Before World War II many companies did not employ married women. The war changed all that, and women became **INVOLVED** in war work. By May 1943, women between the ages of 18 and 45 without children had to help with the war effort. Women drove trains, became motorcycle messengers, fought fires and worked in tank factories. They joined the WRNS (Women's Royal Naval Service) and the WRAF (Women's Royal Air Force). They became drivers and **MECHANICS** with the ATS (Auxiliary Transport Service), planespotters, assisted on anti-aircraft guns and in air force operations rooms, as well as in ARP control centres. They even became **SPIES** working behind enemy lines.

The Women's Voluntary Service (WVS) was founded in 1939 and by the end of 1941 had more than a million volunteers, operating canteens and refuge centres for people in need of help after bombing raids as well as doing vital jobs like collecting scrap metal.

The following is an extract from a speech by the Minister of Labour, Ernest Bevin, trying to persuade women to volunteer for war work:

"I have to tell the women that I cannot offer them a delightful life. They will have to suffer some inconveniences. But I want them to come forward in the spirit of determination to help us through."

The future Queen Elizabeth II served in the ATS during WWII.

Sources – Ernest Bevin's speech was reported in the Manchester Guardian on March 10, 1941

Words to use in your project

consequence *(logical result)*
encounter *(meet)*
occupation *(profession)*

parted *(separated)*
plantation *(area growing crops)*
reap *(cut or harvest grain)*

restrict *(keep within certain limits)*

CHILDREN

Children from London felt the direct effects of living in a country at war. Many were evacuated and **SEPARATED** from their families. If they stayed, they **WITNESSED** the destruction of large parts of London, and in many cases their own homes.

Mavis Cook lived in north London at the beginning of the Blitz and describes her experience of the war:

'One evening we didn't quite make the shelter and I do recall that, and just sort of lying flat in the hallway, or coming out and just sort of lying flat because a bomb had fallen very close to the house. Everything shuddered, you know, glass and everything, you could hear, sort of, the whole house shook... And then my dad said, oh I'll go and see what's happened. And I remember crying and didn't want him to go, and pulling, and saying, no don't go, don't go... And that I think was the first time that I could honestly say I was very frightened. Because, it was just sort of like the tremendous shake of the house...'

Three children left homeless, sit outside the wreckage of their home.

> Source – Extracted from an interview with Mavis Cook conducted by the Museum of London

Women and Children Glossary

allocate	Distribute in shares	**reluctant**	Unwilling
delightful	Charming	**secretary**	A person who does administrative work
munitions	Military weapons, ammunition and stores	**shudder**	Tremble or shake
obstacle	Something that blocks or prevents progress	**tattie**	A name for a potato
		trickle	Flow in a small stream
register	A record or list		

CASE STUDY

Boys of St George's Church of England School, Battersea, digging potatoes.

Tattie picking

During the war, children in the country, including evacuees, were given blue employment cards, which let them work a certain number of hours each term. The farmer and the teacher had to sign the card.

'Tattering' was planting potato crops in the spring. Children were told 'one foot, two foot, tater' so the potatoes would be planted the right distance apart. 'Tattie picking' took place in the autumn when the harvest was ready. Each child was given a section from which to pick potatoes after the spinner had lifted them to the surface. It was back-breaking work, and often very cold and wet.

Margaret Strachan of Aberdeen wrote about her experiences:

"I started tattie picking for 24 shillings (£1.20) a week. The bonus was getting a free bag of the leftover tatties and carrots from the friendly farmers."

See also: Defence 10–11; Destruction 16–17; Significant People 24–25; Weapons 28–29

> Source – BBC Scotland on Film, February 12, 2003

Significant People

The most significant people during this period were political and military leaders. When the war began, Neville Chamberlain was Prime Minister. In May 1940 he resigned when his party refused to support him and Winston Churchill took over. Many people achieved fame as a result of the war, including Neville Barnes Wallis, whose bouncing bomb was used to devastate German industry, and Field Marshal Bernard Montgomery, or 'Monty', who commanded the Eighth Army in North Africa.

WINSTON CHURCHILL

Winston Churchill was born on November 30, 1874. Before he entered politics he had a **DISTINGUISHED** career in the army and as a war **CORRESPONDENT**. He was a keen amateur artist and a writer who later won the Nobel Prize for Literature. In 1900 he stood for Parliament as a Conservative candidate, but in 1904 he joined the Liberal party. He held several key government positions before and during World War I, including President of the Board of Trade, Home Secretary and First Lord of the Admiralty, and he helped to modernise the navy and develop tank warfare. He returned to the Conservative party, and when war was declared he became chairman of the Military Coordinating Committee. Churchill became prime minister on May 10, 1940 at the age of 66. Churchill had many great qualities, but he is probably best remembered for the **INSPIRATIONAL** speeches and public **BROADCASTS** on significant occasions that urged the British people to make even greater efforts.

General Dwight Eisenhower, a renowned American leader during the war wrote:

"An inspirational leader, he seemed to typify Britain's courage and perseverance in adversity and its conservatism in success. He was a man of extraordinarily strong convictions and a master in argument and debate. Completely devoted to winning the war and discharging his responsibility…"

Winston Churchill helped to keep up morale with his famous 'V' for Victory sign.

Sources – Crusade in Europe (1948), Dwight D. Eisenhower

Words to use in your project

allegiance *(loyalty)*
disaster *(event that causes great harm)*
invigorate *(energise)*
notable *(worthy of note)*
printing *(the production of printed matter)*
reconstruct *(build again)*
temperament *(frame of mind)*

SIR ARTHUR 'BOMBER' HARRIS

Sir Arthur Harris, responsible for the massive bombing campaigns in Germany.

Arthur Harris was born in Cheltenham, on April 13, 1892. He held many positions in the RAF, and was promoted to Commander-in-Chief of Bomber Command in 1942. He was in charge of the Allied air campaign until 1945.

Although Harris commanded great respect and loyalty from his crews, his 'saturation' or 'area' bombing technique was questioned even before the end of the war. **BOMBARDING** German cities with 'thousand bomber raids' killed more than 600,000 German civilians, damaged six million homes and flattened historic cities.

In March 1945, Winston Churchill instructed Harris to end area bombing. He explained:

'It seems to me that the moment has come when the question of bombing of German cities simply for the sake of increasing the terror, should be reviewed. Otherwise we shall come into control of an utterly ruined land.'

Harris became a Marshal of the Royal Air Force in 1946 and died on April 5, 1984.

Sources – Winston Churchill, Address to House of Commons, March 28, 1945

Significant People Glossary

adversity	Trouble	**perseverance**	Determination
barge	A large boat	**significant**	Sufficiently great or important to be worthy of attention
conservatism	Opposition to change		
contribute	Take part in	**stature**	Importance or reputation gained by ability or achievement
convictions	Confidence		
impending	Approaching	**typify**	Symbolise
inspirational	Motivating		

See also: The Raids 6–7; After the Raids 14–15; Women and Children 22–23; Art 26–27; Crime 30–31

CASE STUDY

Field Marshal Bernard Montgomery.

'Monty'

Bernard Montgomery was born on November 17, 1887. He fought extensively in World War I, was promoted several times until by 1938 he was commanding the British forces in Palestine. Following the German invasion of north Africa, Montgomery was appointed to command the 195,000 strong Eighth Army.

Montgomery was hugely popular with his troops and returned to the war in Europe, promoted to Field Marshal. He formed a strong military alliance with the US General Eisenhower although the two did not always agree. On May 4, 1945 he accepted the surrender of the German military. Here are his own words about military leadership:

"Military command has always required technical skill and spiritual power and quality. Great commanders have had a profound knowledge of the mechanics of war and the stage-management of battle.."

Source – The Path to Leadership, by Bernard Montgomery (1961)

Many artists and photographers, both famous and unknown, were paid by the Ministry of Information to produce IMAGES of the war and its effects. These pictures and photographs were meant to show what was happening and to record events, but they were also useful for PROPAGANDA, the means by which government used the arts to bolster public morale during the war. Many great POETS and AUTHORS used their talents to record the war, while cartoonists also recorded what they saw.

PAINTINGS

The War Artists' Advisory Committee was set up largely because of Kenneth Clark, who was Director of the National Gallery in London. The committee employed artists to record Britain at war, and eventually took responsibility for the artistic coverage of the war.

At any one time, 30 full-time artists were employed. Specific **COMMISSIONS** were given to another 100 artists, and the work of a further 200 artists was bought. Even more artists worked unofficially.

The Committee commissioned important artists including Henry Moore, Graham Sutherland and Stanley Spencer to record the effects of the war. Other artists, including the painters Anthony Gross and Edward Ardizzone, were sent to places like North Africa, Europe and the Far East where campaigns were being fought. Exhibitions that were organised both in Britain and America aimed to raise morale and to promote Britain's image abroad.

Henry Moore made this painting during the 'Blitz' in London, World War II.

Words to use in your project

acclaim *(greet with praise)*
board *(a group of people who manage a business)*

capacity *(ability to contain or serve)*
discover *(find)*

display *(reveal)*
historic *(relating to history)*

PHOTOGRAPHY

The **DEVASTATION** caused by the Blitz made strong photographic images, at a time when photography was a fairly new way of recording history. The most famous photograph of London in the Blitz was taken from the roof of the Daily Mail offices in Fleet Street in December 1940, by Herbert Mason. It shows the dome of St Paul's Cathedral surrounded by fire and smoke. Despite the devastation all around, St Paul's remained intact and was a symbol of hope and determination for Londoners.

Thousands more photographs of London were taken during the war, including many by George Rodger of *Life* magazine, and Bert Hardy, who worked for the popular magazine *Picture Post*.

Herbert Mason's famous photo of St Paul's during the Blitz, taken in 1940.

Art Glossary

capture Take possession of or control by force

commission Authorise to perform certain duties

coverage Extent to which an event is dealt with

devastate Cause severe shock, distress, grief or destruction

noteworthy Interesting, significant or unusual

propaganda information designed to influence people's opinions

See also: The Blitz 4–5; Evacuation 8–9; Work and Play 20–21; Weapons 28–29

CASE STUDY

Bill Brandt

Bill Brandt was one of the most influential photographers of the last century. He was born in Hamburg, Germany, and worked in Paris and then London. He developed a style of photo-journalism that captured ordinary people in their own settings. His subjects ranged from very wealthy people to those living in the poorest slums. At the height of the Blitz, he took photographs of London and Londoners at different times of the day and night, and even followed crowds into the Underground to escape the bombs. Mark Haworth-Booth, Curator of London's Victoria and Albert Museum, says:

"No other British photographer has made so many memorable photographs as Bill Brandt. He excelled in all fields – social scenes, surrealism, night photography, wartime documentary, landscape, portraiture and the nude."

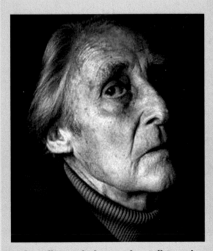

The influential phtographer Bill Brandt.

Source – Mark Haworth-Booth, 2002

Weapons

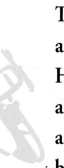

The RAF and the Luftwaffe used a variety of aircraft, fighters and bombers during the war. The RAF flew Spitfire, Defiant, Hurricane, Blenheim, Beaufighter, Lancaster and Gladiator aircraft. The Luftwaffe used Dornier, Heinkel, Messerschmitt and Junkers, including the famous Junkers Ju 87 'Stuka' bomber. The Heinkel He-111 was Germany's primary bomber. Many were shot down by British Spitfires and Hurricanes and it was later used only on NIGHTBOMBING runs.

AIRCRAFTS

The Junkers Ju 88, the Heinkel He111 and the Dornier Do17 were the main bombers used by the Luftwaffe during the Battle of Britain and the Blitz. Although they caused a lot of **DAMAGE,** it was nothing compared to that caused by heavy bombers like the British Lancaster and the American B17 Flying Fortress. Luftwaffe bombers that carried out daylight raids on towns and cities during the Battle of Britain flew in **FORMATION** which was designed to offer maximum **PROTECTION.**

This proved to be of little use, and bombers later flew with fighter **ESCORTS** where possible.

The Messerschmitt BF109 was the German equivalent of the British Spitfire fighter, and the two aircraft were in a technological race until the end of the war. Although the Messerschmitt bomber springs most readily to mind, the Junkers 88 was probably the best German propeller-driven fighter of the war. Sir Arthur Harris wrote about these aircraft in *Bomber Command*:

The Junkers Ju 88 was a four-seat bomber. It was the most versatile German warplane of the World War II era.

"By an almost incredible stroke of luck the pilot of a Junkers 88 mistook England for Germany on July 13th and landed with his aircraft quite undamaged on an airfield in England. It was a Junkers 88 of the latest type and it contained two wholly new instruments for detecting aircraft in the dark."

Source – Arthur Harris, Bomber Command (1947)

Words to use in your project

clatter (rapid succession of sharp noises)
harm (hurt or damage)

inflammable (liable to burn)
ordeal (painful experience)
ruins (remains, wreckage)

widely (extending over a large area)

BOMBS

German incendiary bombs.

Bomber command used three main types of **BOMB**: target indicator, incendiary and high explosive.

At first most German high-explosive bombs ('Sprengbombe') were small-calibre, but gradually bombs of increasing size and weight came into service.

The Luftwaffe also dropped sea mines, fitted with a suitable **DETONATOR**, on British cities where they became universally known as land mines.

In an attempt to make these weapons even more effective, and to defeat the efforts of firefighters, the Germans introduced explosive **CHARGES** that had a **DELAY** of about 7 minutes into the nose or tail of some incendiary bombs.

Joanne Shipway was 17 when war broke out in 1939. This is her account of what it was like to live and work in London during the war:

'Much of what I saw was very traumatic. German bombers not only dropped high explosive, they also dropped incendiaries so I saw horrific injuries caused by both types of bombs.'

Source – Extracted from an interview with Joanne Shipway conducted by the Museum of London

Weapons Glossary

detonator	A device or small sensitive charge used to detonate an explosive	**propeller**	A revolving shaft with spiral blades that makes an aircraft move
explosives	Substances used to cause an explosion	**technological**	Having to do with technology, scientific
incredible	Impossible or difficult to believe; extraordinary	**traumatic**	Emotionally disturbing or distressing

CASE STUDY

A V1 Flying Bomb.

V1/V2

From January 1944, London was bombed very heavily. Though not as bad as the 1940 Blitz, the 'Little Blitz' caused a great deal of destruction and lasted until April 8. This time, the Germans used a more dangerous flying bomb, the V1, as well as the V2 **ROCKET** which travelled faster than the speed of sound.

The V1 was a pilotless plane that flew until its engine ran out of fuel, then came crashing to earth. It carried a **CARGO** of bombs that destroyed all that lay beneath. Londoners called them 'buzz bombs' or 'doodlebugs'.

The following is an extract from an interview with Jim Wood about his experiences as a child during the war:

"The V1s were quite noisy ... They sounded like a motorbike running without a silencer ... and if they stopped overhead you knew they would hit close by."

Source – Interview with Jim Woods, 1987, by the Museum of London

See also: Defence 10–11; Shelters 12–13; Food and Farming 18–19; Women and Children 22–23

Crime

The war created OPPORTUNITIES for looters, conmen and other criminals. Under cover of darkness during the blackout it was easier to commit crimes undetected. Bombed-out houses were impossible to secure, so gangs of looters stole from the ruins of their homes. So many people were being killed by bombs that it was also easier to cover up a murder. Rationing led to black market trade in restricted items like meat, alcohol and clothing. Gangs of juvenile DELINQUENTS also stole from people in public shelters.

LAW AND ORDER

The Blitz created many law and order problems, ranging from looting to murder. Part of the problem was caused by the changes to family life, as fathers went to fight in the war and mothers had to work. City children who had not been evacuated did not always go to school, because the evacuation schemes relocated whole schools and their teachers. This meant that many children were poorly-supervised and they sometimes picked pockets or stole food from allotments and gardens. The *Sussex and Surrey Courier* reported:

> *"Many cases brought before the Juvenile Courts arrive from broken homes. A lack of discipline in such homes was responsible for many of these crimes. The desire for adventure and war stories of deeds at sea, the field, and in the air, led to stealing and destructive behaviour. GANGSTER films and the 'tough' gangster idea also had their influence."*

Even getting away with murder was possible in theory, but the police were aware of this. When the remains on a woman were found in a bombed church in 1942 they investigated further and discovered that she had been murdered. The woman was identified and her husband, Harry Dobkin who was found guilty of murder and hanged.

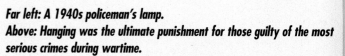

Far left: *A 1940s policeman's lamp.*
Above: *Hanging was the ultimate punishment for those guilty of the most serious crimes during wartime.*

LOOTING AND FRAUD

The government paid money to help those whose homes were destroyed or damaged during bombing raids. It didn't take long for criminals to realise that they could make **FRAUDULENT** claims, as well as start a black market in food and goods that were difficult to obtain during the war. Another form of crime was **PROFITEERING**, in which companies made money out of supplying essential war goods.

LOOTING bombed homes and businesses was considered a terrible crime, but even so in London alone during the first eight weeks of the Blitz 390 cases were reported. The punishment could be death but more usually people were sent to prison. Chief Inspector Percy Datlen reported what happened in Dover after one heavy raid:

'In cases where there are several houses bombed out in one street, the looters have systematically gone through the lot. Carpets have been stripped from the floors… they have even taken away heavy mangles, bedsteads and complete suites of furniture.'

Looters targeted bombed houses and businesses.

Source – Report by Inspector Percy Datlen, Dover CID, April 17, 1942

Crime Glossary

adventure	An unusual and exciting experience	**discover**	Be the first to find out or see
amid	In the middle of	**pickpocket**	A thief who steals from the people's pockets
chaos	A state of confusion and disorder	**upheaval**	Sudden, violent change or disruption
concentrated	Directed toward a common centre		

CASE STUDY

Teenage gangs would steal the bags of people sleeping in shelters like this one at Holborn underground station.

Blackout Gangs

Gangs of teenagers were often blamed for crimes in crowded air-raid shelters. While people tried to sleep they would steal their bags or pick valuables from their pockets. Stealing food including chickens or vegetables from people's gardens was also common. Some burgled houses that were thought to be empty during air raids, though this was risky as it was impossible to tell whether anyone was inside because of the blackout.

On October 24, 1940, when sentencing a 15-year-old boy for burgling a house when its occupants were in a public shelter during an air raid, a magistrate named Colonel Henriques said:

"It is becoming more and more common. It is just playing dirty in wartime."

Source – Colonel Henriques, Clerkenwell Magistrates Court, October 24, 1940.

See also: After the Raids 14–15; Destruction 16–17; Work and Play 20–21; Significant People 24–25

Index

WORLD WAR II & THE BLITZ TIMELINE

Sep 1939
Britain declares war against Germany after invasion of Poland. The first wave of children are evacuated from the cities to the countryside.

Jan 1940
Rationing introduced into Britain. It would last for nearly fourteen years.

May 1940
Winston Churchill becomes Prime Minister of Britain.

Sep 1940
The Blitz begins from September 7th and continues through to 1942, with German air attacks on London, Coventry and other cities.

Dec 1940
German bombing campaign known as the 'Christmas Raids' leads to another wave of evacation of children.

Dec 1941
National Service was enacted. WVS and many other organisations were created.

Jun 1943
Allies begin "round-the-clock" bombing raids over Germany.

Jan 1944
In January more air attacks by Germany were followed by V1 or pilotless flying bombs.

Jun 1944
The D-Day invasion of Europe begins on the beaches of Normandy, northern France.

May 1945
Germany surrenders unconditionally to the Allies. Hitler has already commited suicide.

August 1945
The Americans drop atomic bombs on the cities of Hiroshima and Nagaski in Japan to end WWII.